A CLEARING SPACE
in the MIDDLE *of* BEING

Also by Jeff Hardin:

No Other Kind of World

Small Revolution

Restoring the Narrative

Notes for a Praise Book

Fall Sanctuary

A CLEARING SPACE
in the MIDDLE *of* BEING

Jeff Hardin

LAKE DALLAS, TEXAS

FIRST EDITION

Requests for permission to reprint or reuse material from this work should be sent to:

Permissions
Madville Publishing
PO Box 358
Lake Dallas, TX 75065

Acknowledgements:

Thank you to the journals in which some of these poems previously appeared, sometimes in slightly different versions:

Lake Effect	"Maybe Evident All Along"
Mid-American Review	"Having Questioned the Difference Anything Makes"
New Madrid	"One Another Fate Mostly Forgotten"
Poems & Plays	"Here in a Postmodern World"
	"A View That Wasn't There Before"
Poetry Northwest	"With Only a Vague Outline"

Certain titles echo lines by other poets as follows: "To Leave People and the Rain Behind" and "The Pavanes and Chaconnes That Greet the Ear in Fragments" (John Ashbery); "In the Midst of Looking Out, Thinking about Something Far from Here" and "Our Talk of Things Small and Needing Admiration" (W. S. Merwin); "How Little at Home We Are in the Interpreted World" (Ranier Maria Rilke).

I am grateful to friends old and new who have come alongside me, sharing encouragement, counsel, insight, grace, fellowship, and joy: Mike Turner, Victoria Clausi, Michelle Miller, Becky Yannayon, Kory Wells, Chera Hammons, Gary McDowell, Mark Dawson, Gaylord Brewer, Al Maginnes, and many others.

Special gratitude to David Till, whose office served as my first "clearing space."

Thank you, Starla, for sharing this space—this sacredness—and for enlarging everything I hope to know or imagine. You continually show me who I am.

Cover Design: Jacqueline Davis
Cover Photo: John Sercel
Author Photo: Eli Hardin

ISBN: 978-1-948692-18-2 Paper, 978-1-948692-19-9 ebook
Library of Congress Control Number: 2019937657

friends who cleared my way

Bill Brown
G'anne Harmon
Alice Sanford
Lola White

and

David Till

Contents

A CLEARING SPACE
in the MIDDLE *of* BEING

A THEME THAT MIGHT BE WORKABLE

Isn't it odd how the page you most need
is the page you open the book to, though
seldom is the day you need the one
the calendar grants?
              A whole hillside
of forward-leaning sage (or is it backward-
bowing?) reminds that some things might
be better seen aslant.
              How wonderful anyway
when things line up and have an order
to them, in the way that, moments
after hearing a symphony, one can
stumble, literally, exiting the hall
and someone else reach forth a hand
at just the crucial moment.
              There might be
some parts of a life closing down, never
to be heard from again, no discoveries, no
suggestive images; still, a train is always
leaving a station, even when few are there
to board it.
              One theme that might be workable
is reverie born from being bent toward
the earth, or how the dove-call's presence
serves to anchor down whatever else might
also be occurring.
              And if some moments prove
unlikely, well, consider them able nonetheless
to reverse some earlier premise undiscovered,
though equally mesmerizing, and itself only
a footnote
              in a larger text continually underway.

LEAVING ONE EPISODE TO ENTER ANOTHER

One's own decline may be the nation's
decline, a development insurmountable
for which one feels unprepared and even
unlike one's essential self.
                              To be selfless,
to imagine one's non-existence, gets
both easier and harder with age, like
almost remembering something one
intended to accomplish but which
no concentration now can seem
to summon.
                  One's thoughts send out
root systems in every direction, gripping
down to hold a while longer one's place
upon the earth, to see how much more
more can happen, how much more *less*
will be necessary.
                      All the poem's unnecessary
words are still present, someone may think
and be right, of course, since realistically
few of the words are essential to how
people go about their days, leaving one
episode to enter another, neither serving
as the desired place where, finally, all
moments blaze up into a speaking
voice.
          Though the downspout remains voiceless,
one can listen all night to rain along the roof
drafting a letter no one will read that by
morning's calm will have been absorbed,
every last letter and phoneme of meaning
as gone
              as whatever already begins to arrive.

DIMINISHMENT

So many books on the last chance cart
needing rescued, brightly lit jacket covers
with huge yellow $2 stickers secured
along the spines, obscuring their labored-
over titles.
            Better, perhaps, to remain untitled
in these lives we keep presenting at passing
onlookers too distracted to look up from
status updates and tweets.
                       Alexandria's library,
we're told, went the way of ash, while here
and now there's only here and now and little
worth remembering or going back to
that having lived a while longer might
actually amplify.
              Could be a diminishment
has long been underway, with anything
resembling wisdom more and more
beside the point, not needed, and maybe
not even possible now that words keep
disappearing, fewer choices to fit inside
the screen.
           What happened, tabula rasa,
Dickinson, Basho, Dostoevsky—can we
still dwell in possibility? Will we forget
the sound of water leapt into, the conscience
come again reminding of crimes we can't
escape,
        or have we found a freedom,
finally, not to be tethered to a word's
boundaries, to its demand we live as if,
yes, meaning
             were not meaningless
but lay in abundance everywhere we
look, both titled and untitled, sometimes
slim,
        sometimes arms-filled-unbearably voluminous.

3

AN INSTRESSED MYSTERY STRESSED

Only 8:03, but I've been awake for hours,
and you wouldn't believe how much
goes on in one person's mind, a lot
of it mindless, mind you, but also
whole segments rippling with brilliance,
widening out countless echoes, each
forgotten.
          Through cavernous memory
I'm still crawling, as I used to do
each summer in the Perry Hollow,
silt on my hands and knees, no idea
how far back the cave reached into
the hillside, into the fossil record,
my flashlight angled toward the promise
of a perfect arrowhead.
                        What's more flawed
than wanting perfection, though—one
thought leading to another and rarely
an easy passage, seldom a logical leap,
a long drawn-out *Well...* followed by
a sigh and a lifted coffee cup, a shrug
then a smile then the first dazzled words
of a prayer.
            I pray the Lord my soul
is not some myth without a refund,
some good idea my ancestors thought up
because it sounded more interesting
than *soup* or *sour,* though even if it is
a myth, I'm still pledging my allegiance
to how it takes me to the water's edge,
inviting me to kneel.
                      A heron standing
off the roadside, even in a ditch line,
has become a common image for
the soul: lanky and cumbersome; slow

to lift off; too rarely seen; endangered;
its neck stuck too far toward wherever
flight is taking it.
        On a given day I'm granted
far-fetched pairings (heron and soul; bend
in the road and elbow; teacup and wisdom;
deadbolt and catapult), and I figure
the more irregular, the clumsier they come,
the more the things around me will give
off a hum I might hear and strike out
toward—
        wherever that leads, wherever this ends.

THE GAPS THAT CAN'T BE BROUGHT TOGETHER

Difficult at best to catalogue every influence
exerting pressure on this or that thought,
and probably no one's interested anyway
beyond a cursory acknowledgment of how
easy or natural it is to fall under another
moment's spell.
                    Just as likely we're all illiterate
to what the point is or is building toward,
unable to follow a simple line of reasoning
that begins in what passes for civility
but then becomes indistinguishable from
history's usual conflicts.
                              Bits and pieces
accumulate, though not on the same schedules,
some arriving early, others midway through,
and some after what's been studied intently
has been brushed aside and expunged from
the record completely.
                          Even in Sappho's fragments
some residue exists of her time and place,
the sound of waves, if we listen closely, and
the reach to touch a reader, despite the blank
spaces between words which now, more than
the words, seem to comprise her oeuvre.
                                            One part
of what a thought is is the *thought* of what
it is, another part the gaps that can't be
brought together, not even centuries later
once others have aimed their own thoughts
to fill in the emptiness,
                            attempting a fullness
that may be just another invented notion
to keep us sane, searching, occupied, and alas
reassured—despite the evidence—that what
we know
              won't slide and become, again, unknown.

A VIEW THAT WASN'T THERE BEFORE

In the morning be one person, in the afternoon
another, and thereby escape the usual
constraints of existence, especially in terms
of expectations, not that doing so will
make much difference.
                    A healthy indifference
gives the matter a looseness that allows for
almost anything to enter in and be examined,
even what seems misplaced or beside the point
or strangely missing.
                    So recently found,
a word—like *imbrication*—though having
been an option all along, still can't find
a way into a conversation without sounding
ridiculous, and that's just one word, and
who can say how many more words might
appear.
                  REM says, "I came to disappear,"
which seems an echo of the Apostle Paul
saying one has to die to self, an idea certainly
not new but still revolutionary and ultimately
pragmatic.
                  The truth is what doesn't work
has a beauty, too, even a usefulness, and
often opens up a view that wasn't there
before, as when a train passes and in its
aftermath a plastic bag is wind-caught
into a beautiful nowhere
                    that could lead anywhere—
into this or that realm, into another season,
into a context where meanings multiply,
into a conversation
                  where no one has to speak.

AUSTERITY AND WHOLENESS IN THE IMMANENT DAY

Always the question of what to do
with too many abstractions, whether
to agree they are shadows of things
or whether they are light giving insight
into what things are.
          What things *aren't*
is always a guess or, if not always, then
half the time, which is itself a guess,
or maybe a conjecture, and then only
a midpoint on the way to somewhere
else undetermined.
          Not that I've determined
how best to describe or to authenticate
"the ideal," but I've pretty much ruled out
standing alone on bridges like that guy
in Munch's painting and not because
I dislike crossing over or fear the roiling
in my head but because, yes, bridges
sometimes fall.
          Early and eager I rise
and sometimes sense austerity in
the rendering of another moment
gathered and released as if a dream
stepped out of or stepped into full
of bird flight.
          A snail's trail—
what else in the world can claim to be
as overlooked or followed less, as little
mentioned or mythologized, as un-
mimicked, when, if studied closely,
it appears to be dividing the earth
into two halves.
          A certain wholeness
feels more or less immanent each day,

especially when fireflies show up,
moving backwards among tree branches,
giving the air the slip—and the ceiling
of what can be thought about begins
to swirl.

      Mostly, I prefer solid ground,
though I admit to being swept away,
enamored by all that's implausible and
dangling off the edges of anything I say,
not paying much mind but thinking it all
inevitable anyway, and maybe it is
or is likely—as likely as *oleander* being
the next word
               right after I am wordless.

HAVING QUESTIONED THE DIFFERENCE
ANYTHING MAKES

One idea I had fit nowhere neatly,
so I took it out into the sun,
thinking the warmth would help,
but when that did no good,
I took it up a hill and left it
for dead.
        Aside from that, I live
quite peaceably non-assertively
and don't ask for or expect too much,
having questioned the difference
anything really makes to what already
is.
      Of what once was or might be
we speak of often but seldom reach
conclusions, not that they would
be definitive or a way out of some
unease but that they remind us
of what is possible, even if
tentative.
        The taste of the eternal,
I heard someone say, is increasingly
absent in our words, to which I
wanted to add, "So is *to dwell*,
so is *a wave along the sand*, so is
*a child's lofty sky on a sketch pad
soon erased*."
        Evenings I am drawn
by a light steered toward me in
a hawk's cry, an implied assertion
it makes good sense not to study
too closely but to wander around
inside.
      A momentum takes me outside
myself sometimes, though this sense

of being a soul is hard to explain,
as anything is mostly a few words
battered together to make a spark
in a dry place, a few leaves worrying
the ground
            so far from the sweep of the sky.

ONE WORD SETTING FORTH REVERBERATIONS

Because Salma Hayek is whispering
each word—that's my response
when asked why anyone would want
to read this poem. It's not true,
but I figure it'll take some time,
maybe all the way to the end,
before a reader finds out he's
been duped.
    Misleading information
isn't always a bad thing, since
some of the time it keeps one
interested and other times leads
down a road with a guava tree
or an old man on his porch tossing
up a nod, a wave.
    As greetings go,
I prefer a neighbor handing me
apples in a bucket or jasmine leaves,
harmonica music to do a little
side-step dance to, nothing fancy,
just quirky and worth a smile,
though I promise not to get too
carried away and embarrass myself
like usual.
    Not that I'm an advocate
of the unusual, the out-of-nowhere,
couldn't-see-coming-in-a hundred-
years swerve of logic, but I'm
beginning to think our best thinking
doesn't go down a list but loves
more the scattershot approach,
how the mind can move from wren
to woodsmoke, from bric-a-brac
to Yalta.
    I love, though, how when I

hear or see the words *midway through*,
I can't help but hear Dante's poem,
and I wonder what happens to souls
who hear too many echoes, one
word setting forth reverberations
back through centuries of thought,
what that must do to a person, even
standing in the grocery line hearing
the word *disturb*.
                The universe,
dare I say, has its own story to tell,
its own flung-out, wide-around-
the-edges narrative a lifetime's just
a sliver of, just as Monet's best version
gets only a glimpse of what a lily really
is to the moment it sturdies itself forth
inside a thought
                becoming now eternal.

TETHERED TO NOTHING BUT A VEERING
TOWARD SOMETHING ELSE

Living a hundred years seems one way out of
the ecstatic moment and also a way to admire
many things from afar, with less memory for
why they mattered—not a bad thing, given
all one has witnessed, or heard, or heard of
and retained.
              Names are so many I lose
them like leaves, and they overlap, letters
or syllables laid down over each other,
making a mishmash, an intoxication of
incoherence and caution when meeting friends
in the supermarket.
              Instead of "How are you?"
I want to ask "What does your presence mean?"
or "What are you becoming, in light of all
the light you've pulled inside yourself?"
              I need less
proof these days to point me in directions which,
before, I steered away from, or thought I did,
believing I was choosing where to step or stray,
when to open a door, how long to linger at
the edge of a crowd before deciding no one
cared I was present.
              I am here, I guess,
as much as I've been anywhere, sometimes
adding a whistle to the air, something faint
only my angel hears, and not a likely tune
or one I promise to remember, mostly full
of new beginnings, starts that idle a while
around a note, tethered to nothing but a veering
into something else.
              Like one year into another
or words into hope, into truth, or how
bitterness turns to letting go, then to joy,

a kind of lifting-off the spirit feels which
seems silly when explained, attempting to
recreate the torque of the sensation, part mind
being unhinged, part canvas with nothing on it,
part being ineligible
                    but showing up anyway.

A WANDERINGLY VAST PLACE TO BE

In this movement from one dislocation
toward another, I've begun to admit
my fealty to the one in his chair dozing
in some immaculate dream no one dares
stir the edges of, snow falling beneath
the undersides of his lids.
                              Beginnings
seem profound at first, smooth as any
stream below the hills, then turn toward
some too-close foreground full of clover
—oh which leaf to pick and not become
the poorer?
                    Unimportance being a credo
has led me so far into wider nowheres
than I would have found otherwise,
"I" being a wanderingly vast place
to be, not at all local, as I had suspected,
but a kind of receptivity astonishingly
astute, able to sense that moment
the rain-ring on the pond reaches
the end of its opening eye.
                                    Impossible
I'm possible, yet here I am, skeptical
of *being*, unsure how best to lean it
in directions that won't be seen as
incidental.
                    I suppose a guess gets
as close as any answer can or makes
a point that logic cannot hold, an echo
further down inside a kettledrum
inspection cannot find or fathom
but imagines as a milieu everywhere
moved through, mine at least,
nothing less than *minded*, thus
mended—as in the way time, grown

sublime, comes to mean the meaning
it reaches ever toward,
                                unable to behold.

A WALK ONE IS ALWAYS HAVING WITH ONESELF

Back at the beginning, someone must
have stood around and wondered
what next, the others going about
the tasks at hand, unconcerned
a silence was pressing in from all
directions.
           Two roads apparently diverged,
a poet told us, but wasn't his point
that they, essentially, were one road
and the mind, being divided, attempts
to console itself with *what ifs*
and longings, throwing in autumn's
yellows to tinge the moment with
nostalgia.
           "And ye shall be satisfied
therewith," some prophet said once
whose name meant "worshipper
of Yahweh," but people were living
off the land back then, in need of
corn and wine and seemingly
always under threat of being
driven into barren and desolate
places.
           Everyone misplaces
a reason or two, can't remember
when or why or how the path
became an upward-turning-toward-
and-into sunlight sifted through a
million leaves.
           "The one who has
arrived," Canetti told us, "has a long
way to go," which is cause to keep
in motion, I suppose, the soul
and body weaving in and out

of one another in their constant
conversation.

    If it ever gets quiet
in my head; if the silence becomes
a space of no light skimming stones
I bend to put inside my pocket,
that's when I'll be a hollowness,
God forbid, nothing more can
fill.
  Not that the emptiness
of a bird feeder matters much,
for it's a soaring sky-full country,
but I take the feeder down,
replenish it with sugar water,
my small part in the pantomime,
one clear action I know is given me
to do—
    to feel how far it feels *to be.*

TO LEAVE PEOPLE AND THE RAIN BEHIND

My tabulations have run amok
so that, without thinking, I include
Harold Bloom and the cardinal
off the porch, and that's when I know
things aren't adding up.
                 If I subtract
the kitchen table, the fireplace, the wren
from all my conversations, to whom
will I speak then, and who will be
nearby, lost in her own nostalgia,
perhaps shivering and dreamy-eyed,
staring out the window?
                 A door left
open solves some problems, maybe the ones
that would have solved themselves anyway,
but so many others resemble wheat stalks
too numerous to gather beneath a sky
only dreaming could invent.
                 Waking,
I tell myself "to leave people and the rain
behind," a snippet from Ashbery not at all
connected to anything but all the more
lovely for being ludicrous, for I adore
people wrestling umbrellas, and rain
I find enchanting, especially if one has
nowhere really to be and can meander
among puddles filling.
                 Some days I'm drained
from talking and thinking and pointing
at what happens as if that's the last
headscarf ever to be wind-caught
in a pantomime of irreducible undulations
or the final basket of apples on a table,
a not-quite loud enough still-life simple
with redness,
                 toward which winds once blew.

THE MIND MARKING OUT A CLEARING SPACE

It's the people who look like mannequins
you have to be leery of; and then
when one walks in, I do little more
than stare, though I try really hard
to act like I'm reading a great book
from which I have to look up
perplexed.
      Some things come clear
but clarify only a need for more
clarity, the same as when the minute
hand leaps forward but hasn't
gone anywhere more distinguishable
than where it just was.
      There is
a stream of light on summer evenings
stippling down through oak leaves,
touching too many places on earth
for one weary man alone to walk,
meditating.
      A mind given to speculation
tempts the void, is up to fundamental
shenanigans the id doesn't exactly
approve of, the mind marking out
a clearing space in the middle of
being, a preview of eternity, time's
lack
    experienced in its fullness.

MAYBE EVIDENT ALL ALONG

What our hometowns solved wasn't
a question we were asking anyway,
and once we'd found new places
that made us feel like pilgrims,
that's when we finally got around
to jotting down ideas in notebooks
we've since lost.
    Lately I've found
a renewed curiosity for all things
indifferent, for how the dog doesn't
stir when I approach, for how
twigs fall at my feet as if the tree,
or fate, were having its own
vivid adventure and I were just
some bystander.
    Innocent? one asks,
yet that's an oversimplification
of how any one moment or action
is really just an accrual of deletions,
adjustments, delays, and concessions
too numerous to map out into any
fathomable sequence.
    Randomness
is something I've grown to trust,
believing it not to be the opposite
of order but a servant of some
larger frame or panorama I would
not reach on my own, so that when
some stray word enters the conversation,
I say we let it sing even if it seems
distracting or off course.
    Of course,
any discourse, any stumble-along
through the moonlight on the path
late-night-from-nowhere to some

where or *when* or *maybe evident*
all along keeps making itself up
in desperation because the ending
that would tie it all together cannot
be imagined.

      Realistically, the facts
do add a shading, a dimension,
to what's known or can be, but when
one says *prairie sky* or *tentless* or
quickening stream around a rock,
it's more a mood than a notation,
for anywhere in the world one
looks

     something else unseen appears.

AN ANSWER TO SOMEONE I MIGHT TRY TO BECOME

My inferences are sometimes like
what I imagine shock treatments
produce, cells in one part of
the brain once adored now
disappeared
            or at least so lessened
their sparks are low-wicked affairs
and I have to learn how to speak
again among my own kind.
From available criteria, I deduce
a calm day put in the mail without
a stamp or a postmark
                  was returned,
never reached me here where I sit
out back trying my best to be alive
but without much pollination,
just some trembling over what
might be ponderable,
                  just not by me.
Like when I hear Eva Cassidy sing
"Time After Time," and there must be
some gaping hole in an already
gaping hole in the cosmos
              without
all the glorious songs she would have
sung if her own cells hadn't been
outsung
       so that so much now
sounds like chatter in comparison.
Then a train passes about which
I wasn't inquiring,
           but it serves
as an answer of sorts to someone
I might one day become when

I've grown less eager for reward
and want simply to watch what
happens right in front of me.
                              Or
have I considered how no one can
pull forth every honeysuckle silk
down the fencerow and, even if
someone could, what that might
imply just before signing one's
name?
        How, then, get pomegranates
into the next conversation, which
could only improve outcomes,
even what doesn't come to pass
or what might turn out to be a new
parable unfolding, still instructive
but this time with a thousand
seeds
        bursting seismic on the tongue.

HAVING BROKEN FROM THE PATH TO FIND
ANOTHER

I can't say when it was when the planes
started overhead, but we began to look up
a few times a day, off into the distance,
pre-occupied or occupied, and to what
we were adhering thereafter no one knows
for sure, though it's reasonable to conclude
a heaviness had set in.
                              I'd been thinking
about undersides versus overviews,
believing myself capable of the latter
but living a captive of the former,
wondering, for instance, what a leaf was
carrying along I couldn't see and what, too,
it most resembled, what it most would
speak, should someone come alongside
and listen.
                  Not that I have an imagination
correctly grammarized or able to inhabit
the blue of water or the coming-to-be
concretions of a pearl or the mind of
an ant crawling the folds of a caryatid,
but I'm available if such a moment comes
to pass.
              How lilies on the pond ready
their faces to hold up whatever scrambles
into place, themselves an exhalation come
up from the depths, fixed upon the scene—
then I wonder how anyone comes along
and gets to be the one who gets to see them
and becomes then their advocate, having
broken from the path to find another
moment's distillation, maybe bidden,
maybe benediction, maybe nowhere else
to go back to.

The reeds, too, are a marvel,
a prologue worth reading even if the wind
makes them founder a bit, each slender
story line entwined though still in movement
to the point that one might as well sit down
and rest a while, consonant with not knowing
any more than what the reeds—lilting,
listing—begin to list,
                    begin to lean against . . .

HERE IN A POSTMODERN WORLD

As for concerns, I have them for
a while and then misplace them
in the way a question continues
unanswered and unlocated on
a misremembered page of Balzac
or Proust, and who has the energy
to go looking for it after all these
years, having prospered without it
to some degree.
          I'm convinced
even ticket sellers at the opera
can't keep track of every seat
and just want to wave somebody in
off the street who wasn't planning
on an aria but might be changed forever,
if that sort of thing still happens
in a postmodern world, and who's
to say it can't since who's to say
anything anymore?
          I'm probably
a disreputable source for some sorts
of information—aardvarks or string
theory, the width or circumference
of echoes—but I'm your guy if
you wish to marvel at what didn't
happen but could have if only
a few more people had gotten together
to talk through the night, asking
whether sonnet output increases
or decreases when the moon is
waxing or waning.
          Maybe it's not
concerns I have but notions lacking
intensity, a yard full of fireflies too

drowsy to lift from sycamore leaves,
though who can blame them.
                              Not I
as I wait on the porch without a single
mandate or hint of truth to offer up,
having cleared my throat all these years
for what amounts to a whisper and then
not even that
                    since I'm keeping it to myself.

HOW LITTLE AT HOME WE ARE IN THE INTERPRETED WORLD

I asked you what you kept hidden,
and you said some things had been
hidden so long you'd forgotten
where to look for them, had given
them back to the void and then
apologized for saying "the void"
because who really says that except
the pretentious or someone fresh out
of philosophy class or recovering from
reading Kafka.
                    I keep things hidden
in books, I said, old handwritten
notes from the deceased I come
across by accident and then take
a minute to sit remembering,
sometimes a mundane instruction
suddenly become prophetic, as if
the seeds were all along inside
the words, a mention of leaves
cascading downward too clichéd
to bear.
          I think I've always feared
echoes, you said—
                    (feared echoes, I said)
perhaps because they lie, you said,
in their promise that a voice returns
from out there—
                    (out there? I asked)—
or in here, you said, touching
a place to signify your heart
as I sat hearing leaves nervous
along, not knowing from where
or why, and this day, like any day,

like any word, always answering
another
        not given to us to know.

IN THE MIDST OF LOOKING OUT, THINKING ABOUT SOMETHING FAR FROM HERE

We walked out into our yards, surveying
the damage of an afternoon's quiet
of limbs along the ground, mole tunnels
a meritocracy even the cat conceded to
and slunk around, we being dreamers
at one time, rejoicing even in the fact
of breathing.
          All of this what-used-to-be
occurred within the bounds of its own
supposedness, as when a piece of driftwood,
once it is witnessed, has to be followed
until it gets caught in roots or slides slow
around the bend, small drama of enormity
unfolding inside its own time.
               What I
might have expected, though, cannot *be*
followed, an expectation being a semblance
of what the mind can't fully picture so that
whatever happens seems as acceptable as
what doesn't, both originating from the same
source anyway.
          Anyway, some of the limbs
we picked up and carried to a pile three years
still unburned, all the cast-offs of oaks
and the one beech and two sycamores
and maybe something of our own lives too,
year after year, both of us working amid
unspoken dialogues carried on with former selves
that are really beginningless,
               neverendingly
interrupting our current selves and pointing
where next to look, where next to walk—

each moment hit or miss—today on grass
like a carpet, tomorrow ankle-deep down
a hole wider than first suspected,
                              deeper too.

OBSERVATIONS COMPOSED AT SOME REMOVE

At one remove, maybe two, I stand
and look upon my life, a too casual
thing, not worth much except that
sometimes I'm the antithesis to those
around me, who claim confusion
and disinterest but admit to waiting
on a package, ordered a while back,
the confirmation notice already having
been emailed.
         Inscrutable days follow
one after another, and while I'd hoped
to enter a cathedral, I find instead
a coffee shop, a leaf-strewn patio
of somnolent voices overheard trying
to get back to some former attitudinal
position less like the chatter sadly
everywhere else.
         But the matter, when
understood, ought to come to something
and not just a secret to tell the self,
since the self is only another secret
and not even one reliable, certainly
not trustworthy.
         Then again it may be
the matter's composed as much of one's
disinterests as of one's interests, or is it
a blurring of both, or one set in relief
against the other, or some conversation
between the two to which one has to
listen all the more intently, intensely,
even conspiratorially, not trusting either
lest one be deceived.
         The months go by
nonetheless, summer coming to an end,
if not to a resolution, coming to something

unapproachable even as one gets nearer
and nearer, pressing onward as the verse
says to do, though up ahead be detours
and re-routings and enemies come from
the undergrowth, wielding stones and insults,
and every door closed and locked, no dove
on the power lines,
                              flushed off years ago.

IN THE ABSENCE OF A RECOGNIZABLE AGENDA

After a while we have to ask
just how much exposure to
mutability we need—is there
a normal amount beyond which
a simple trip to the park turns
embarrassingly too attentive
and/or overreactive?
              Enchantment—
there's an outmoded notion not too
many admit to or adhere to—though,
were it a town, it would be down
one of those roads off an interstate
winding through corn fields
in wartime.
              Ever think small lives
were meant to stay that way,
being their most effective by
all the questions they never think
to ask?
           Lately, what's inconceivable
sits like a boulder in the streambed,
drawing, supposedly, the wilderness
around it, but at least we can jump
from it into a summons of cool water
and drift.
            No agenda sounds fine,
another morning, another evening,
the mind's countless cantilevers
contending with the breeze across
the porch and how the moment
cannot last but seems expansive
anyway, leaning past the impatiens;
and even if one stood, stepped
from the porch, and started
walking,
                one still would not arrive.

OUR TALK OF THINGS SMALL AND NEEDING
   ADMIRATION

It's possible he was an anarchist,
the subdued kind. What he didn't say
wedged its way into conversations,
gazelle leaps in the midst of things
small and needing admiration. Some
called him foolhardy but in his presence
became tongue-tied, like anyone would
walking about on terra firma or looking
out train windows, longing for some
place other to live.
                    One wonders what
responsibility comes with having thoughts
at odds with prevailing ideas—is there
a path set forth, irreversible, down which
not to proceed would in no way negate
yet mysteriously, inevitably make more
apparent?
                Surely some are called but
never answer or lose focus; some springs
rise to ride the ground only to sink
a few feet away, never to be seen
again, and who knows what reward
such momentary being allows someone
dipping a hand into the flow, feeling
the cool.
                Who knows, though,
what anyone else is saying, what anyone
else is hearing themselves say, which
may sound nothing like what others
hear and none of it what needs to be
said, be heard, as if always waking
to November when May is what puts
the mind at ease, its mornings ample
and languishing in nothing that feels

like despair or apology but like
a precedent, hinting toward vastness
before settling
            into this smallest joy.

A MOMENTUM OF MORNING LIGHT

The memories, of course, were in past tense,
which made them easier to deal with since
they were, in theory, farther away, and
the voice they offered sounded like cicada
swirls from a yard several houses over during
a party in which half the people invited didn't
show up.
        I know I, for one, look forward to
going back, all those days I spent wandering
my neighborhood, waving at someone I didn't
know on her porch or the time I cut through
a field because it seemed like a shortcut,
except that it wound farther into itself, and I
ended up beneath the width of an oak not seen
up close, which had a rope hanging down,
frayed at the end, and I still don't know what
to make of that.
        Just to be here, to think about
anything—snow on a neighbor's hillside,
the unlikelihood some pebbles will ever be
held—seems like a strange but accidental
pleasure I've been invited to attend, the result
of which is that I've lain aside incredulities,
some at least, and while morning light builds
momentum, I sense a similar motion inside
to which I've grown agreeable, if not altogether
impatient for.
        The new ways are not the old,
though the old ways, too, were often just
a few steps out of the tavern, edging too close
to a busy highway; one can pick neither, in truth,
when the purpose is to reach conclusions
disprovable or to find a pattern less wracked
with guilt or to move from the vestibule

into the grand room where the entertainment
may not be worth the trip.
                              "But where's
the template?" someone asked, and another
said, "In the word contemplate," and I've
long thought how sustaining that answer
has become, though it's true we are surrounded
by signifiers, billboards, rabble-dreaming
spokespersons, too many empty easels, but
the thing to remember is that you can always
start in one direction and end up somewhere else,
and there'll still be someone to wave you in,
a fellowship of sorts, a word spoken that puts
you back on that path through corn rows you
haven't thought of in years but now see yourself
wandering,
                 pulling back husks, then silks . . .

THE PAVANES AND CHACONNES THAT GREET THE EAR IN FRAGMENTS

Some sense—just a little—insinuates itself
into the scene so that for a moment
the principle participants get a glimpse
of what they're doing, and it's spirited
and revolutionary, though no one can
say for sure until time enough has
passed, and no one knows how long
that might be.
                        Or everyone involved,
it may be determined, might turn out
to be only silhouettes, wavering—oh,
listen, we could pause to eavesdrop on
a woman picking trillium and remember
how it's the taller grasses we get lost in,
not having memorized the indigo bunting's
song, though not for lack of time, not for
lack of wanting to know.
                        And a few
we encounter openly talk to existence
and, for all we know, receive answers,
or late notices, or invitations to run off
in rickshaws down cobblestone streets
curving into yellow light mesmerizingly
unending.
                        All along someone should
be taking notes, compiling testimonies,
cataloguing liquescent motions and sudden
gasps from crowds. Who's responsible here?
What should be done? How mortal or
immortal is anyone in garments made
of memory, these conversations becoming
solitudes?
                        So many misgivings to reflect
upon, shadows in the splendor, rain drops

tugging a pond beyond its eastward gaze,
a whole day reconstructed out of soarings
abandoned before their zenith, though
let's agree we are taken right out of these
days as we know them, not knowing
we don't know them fully, not all of them,
not for long,

               certainly not for long enough.

NO SUCH THING AS HOMELAND

That all the blur of me is hurtling
nonstop through the galaxy
I haven't got a hold on just yet,
but I send tidings nonetheless
from where I currently am,
just this side of a winter
storm.   As all the greats do,
I keep studying circumference—
how picturesque—though
I'm quick to admit flagrant,
flapping butterfly wings
around a daisy pretty much
stop me on the path.
                        Call me
an outward-moving narrative
circling back again to learn
again what more to gain,
what else to gather up
and strain to carry toward
the unknown twists and turns
I still will not be ready
to believe.
            Like the peacock
in the road I hit one time.
Like when I hear a bit
of wisdom secondhand.
Like how a hay bale in a field
is there one day and then
the next day no one, yet again,
is climbing it.
                        What kind
of inventory it must take
to goad us from the ordinary,
shopworn, humdrum thoughts

mistaken for companions we
spend our days with, foreheads
leaned against windows, no
chorus inside.
        Remember how
a trail led through the night
to end up at a river, some
defiance in the moonlight's
staying where it was, no
matter what was tossed
to unsettle it, there being
no such thing as *homeland*,
only the far-reaching eloquence
of reminiscences
                not present yet.

REGARD

My regarding techniques are awash,
too much repetition,
                    or else I've lost
my study habits when it comes
to being still beneath a willow,
expecting light to goldfinch out
of nothingness, which sometimes
happens anyway.
                    Lately I've wondered
whether intuition is counterintuitive,
just one big *otherwise* to everything
I try to contemplate,
                  as though
I've walked out the front door
and ended up out back among
calla lilies deep enough to bury
thoughts of death in.
                 And now's
as good a time as any to announce
another answer no one will remember
decades hence,
               the sound of *susurration*,
for starters, or how an open window
sorely goes unnoticed until the day
it isn't.
          One day and then another,
each a kind of wadded up draft
tossed aside, full of stalled equations
and a few notes Thelonius Monk
tried to give away, a darkened
basement of nodders but no takers.
What, anyway, would it mean
to behold what can't be held,
to stand back from it, whatever
it is—

fallen shed, thread of light
sewn through leaves, unsaid words
on the air between any two people
chosen at random.
                    It means that
nothing *can be* random, that a
memory of moon along a window-
sill prompts another memory
of peacocks.
                    It means you're still
wandering, as they did, calling
out, heard from some place
different each time—that voice
that sounds like *help! help!*—
always another street over, but
still the same
                    small neighborhood.

NOTHING WITHHELD TO ANYONE LOOKING

One hesitation—the annuls say it
takes just one—and then the fate
you wanted passes on to someone
else while you're left looking on,
wishing you'd made the call an hour
earlier.
      Only later can you appreciate
how some days grant picturesque
vineyards not listed in a guidebook
and other days even Proust throws
up his hands at the enormity inside
a raindrop.
      The image of snow
rising might be one kind of healing,
but so many such images exist—
none withheld to anyone looking—
that the need to *be* healed may be
only a myth.
      Based on a true story
the movie advertisements claim,
and so many have been led astray
by partial truths leading over
terrain they were ill-equipped to
navigate.
      Going roundabout wherever
was how my father drove the county
backroads, looking for nothing
in particular, salving something
inside himself, I guess, stopping
on wooden bridges to watch
the creekflow full of leaves
drawn slow and silent around
the bend.
      Does *thought* straighten
the mess of the mind, or does it

add to the roiling toil of juts
and shifts, the compacted expanses
loitering and multiple and mostly
too subtle to remember once they've
been touched?
                    Part of hearing
takes us across to what we're listening
for, but then another part stays back,
recounting old sums and their seasons
of discontent, how, having read
a sentence just once, the self now
undoes itself,
                    readying for a re-do.

ALONG WITH THE FLOW

Another day's ruse sets in and I follow,
though, mostly, I'm disbelieving
and refuse to go along with anything,
loving the at-oddsness I've spent
years perfecting.
                        When generous,
a neighbor shows up at a widow's,
repairs a section of fence so cows
won't run amok, and no one I know
calls that a ruse, though a few more
could stand to get duped like that,
including myself.
                        Or else get dumped
out of one life into another, maybe
one where iris is currency or where
a porch light flipping on/off/on/off
is a word we don't know yet but
sense coming true.
                        Right now, at least,
most people I know have yet to be stolen,
are not extinct, their million conversations
not vapor, unremembered, not shaken
out to dust.
                        Of all I don't know the part
I don't get is knowing I can't know
what I won't ever know, even though
I'm open and wholehearted seeking,
waiting at times.
                        I go along with that, O ruse,
but I won't say I'm finished, for I'm thieving
and sneaky and cryptically discreet; I won't
say what I've taken but keep it close by for
the day of our reckoning, for even this one
thought
                        is tipping the balance my way.

AFTER A WHILE I JUST GOT UP AND TOOK A WALK

to be among tall grasses nuzzling light
which, in solitary moments, I've imagined
my own mind doing, though what that might
look like could be endless.
                              I'm not in my
own life at times, a kind of hush cast over
the next steps taken—maybe that's what
people mean when they say *devout* or sense
some calm come upon them within a moment
unexplainably including the self which is
itself unexplainable.
                        I don't need an answer,
or I won't be anxious when provocations
begin to undermine the nouns and verbs I
hold in high esteem; for while I stand on hills
and look down, taking in a field's slow motions,
I lean toward thinking some healing is already
underway.
            Of course, why I needed to get up
in the first place might as well go without saying,
being either unknown or partially known or too
tremendous to approach, as so many things are,
as you and I and cloud and moon are unapproachable,
and the river past the trees is,
                                    and the vigils of wrens.

TO ASK MAY BE THE ONLY ANSWER

He gave his life to being studious, forgetting
most of what, at the time, he found
fascinating.
     Truth was, much that was dull
occupied his thinking, too: the angle of a straw
beside a cup of tea; the creak of a door
swinging open.
      His own cells closing down
seemed like he imagined it would
one day happen, at just the moment things
began to look up, a success or two at last
arriving.
    Do answers or questions depart,
or do they infold into one another
so that to touch the face of one requires
a tenderness of letting go, accepting that
to ask, in the first place, may be the only
answer.
    How to move then past the question
of why what happens happens and why
what doesn't doesn't and then why none of it
makes sense.
    More and more, nonsense
has the upper hand and mocks the little faith
he's spent a lifetime working out in fear
and trembling.
     His voice, though, holds a stillness
hard to fathom that even he has been surprised
to hear and finds a comfort in, a fact the mind
for all it knows and thinks it knows and doesn't
know
   can't explain, hushed at last before the unknown.

WITH ONLY A VAGUE OUTLINE

Afternoons I just get tired of the wind
against my face, adding or subtracting—
I'm not sure which—so I get up from
the porch and head inside.
                    I'm sure I'm not
the only voice to wonder whether I'm living
in a Victorian novel, walking the grounds
and worried about my place; or whether
I, too, will awaken one day with something
hideous upon my chest.
                  In the brain's recesses
I figure anyone looking earnestly long enough
will happen upon an orchard with a few
ripe peaches and, sitting down, taste one,
then another until, growing sated, the day
simply falls away.
              Who needs remembrance
anyway, so much absence trying to be presence
and vice versa, as though some vague outline
were trying to outdo the story line's arc,
as though a windowsill could be confused
for a window.
          Moving from one suggestion
to another, from place to place, may be
transience at work, but even if problematic,
it also sometimes turns epic.
                A single haiku,
let's assume, could redirect an empire or
set in motion outlandish blessings or bring
a pond to stillness thereby affecting other
stillnesses, both animal and human, and
perhaps even *thirst* itself, a well down which
one stares
          waiting to hear the end of hearing.

WHAT GETS FOUND AND LIVED WITH LONG
  ENOUGH

In one part of my brain, I need
to be doing one thing—giving
a lecture on the beauty and
usefulness of absolute phrases—
and in another part I need to be
writing this poem.
        My thoughts, though,
flame up like a thousand sprouts of
greenly-quiet and breeze-clenched
grass at my feet, though a charismatic
storm draws near.
        Think of Van Gogh
before those fields of swirling skies,
what *philosophy* a color might be,
receiving to itself the marvels of light
cascading, flowing, the first September
days of yet another year, the haunting
inside a cathedral formed from clouds
and wind.
        Form, itself, may simply
be the fate, the shape, of what gets
found and lived with long enough
to hear a music, a memory of something
more or something less that might have
been, the secret a secret keeps, even
from itself.
        As when, looking through
reading glasses, I seem to hold a pen
at one angle, refracted, wavering,
circling the shapes of letters; and then
I look up at the reddish hue between
the bent and billowing hackberry trunks,
the horizon burning with a note Handel
reached for but missed.

And I attempt—
amid my own acceleration of cells, amid
the spaces between my thoughts—to trace
the edges of a word onto a page, all I can
really do, being enamored a single word
exists, how it leaps about trembling and
prodigal
          inside the only home it is becoming.

THE COMING TOGETHER OF MANY INTERSECTIONS

Once a day arrives, what is there to do
except to walk out into it—the only
day in existence—as if existence were
just one more thing among others
unexplainable.
         Of course, what's explainable
is merely the coming together of many
intersections all at once from countless
directions so that all one can do is be
content to stand still, everything flowing
inward.
         Such an extraordinary outward
display of affection for one's presence in
the world as others have gone elsewhere
can seem insensitive if not self-absorbed,
but the desire to lift one's arms and praise
the sun's warmth can be overwhelming
and hard to suppress.
         The need to nurture,
to maintain, to keep alive a faint memory
that never assumed a central role in one's
formation suggests one might have come
to be another self entirely had certain
moments not been focused on so often
or exclusively.
         Mystery itself is inclusive,
allowing each thing—hay bale, aster,
robin's egg, train whistle, open window—
to be suffused with an inwardness
of questions asked and answered
then kept secret.
         What gets revealed
isn't always what one searched for

but what one found along the way,
not thinking of how a leaf scuttling
past
    brings one wholly into the present.

THE REMAINDER AFTER THE PROBLEM IS SOLVED

The song says, "Tuesday's gone with
the wind," but it's Saturday, at least
in my world, even if the sycamore's
silence feels like Wednesday, cold
and rainy.
        Where have the months
disappeared to—that usual question
no one expects an answer to, but
isn't the wistfulness of asking it
ever well-fitting?
        I figure some
of what I'm feeling is connected
to those problems with remainders,
some left-out, left-over outcast
number, though the problem's been
"solved," the teacher eager to move on
to new material.
        It's the immaterial
that's always concerned me,
Stafford saying, "How you breathe,"
how long a person might live inside
that singular, exquisite phrase, its
always-arriving, ever-deepening
epiphany.
        "How you think," I add,
wondering where the supercollider is
for the splitting of thoughts, how much
energy must still exist inside "Let…"
followed by "there" followed by "be,"
an everywhere-sacred explosion
of light.
        I wonder, ponder, wander
along some back corner edge of my
life, sensing some secret will be

revealed only to me, maybe a note
no song has yet to find, which,
having taken in, hummed to myself,
I breathe back into
                  willows overflowing.

AS A BEGINNING OR ENDING HAS A QUALITY

How find the way to *living*,
the man, it seemed, was trying
to say, though not in those exact
words, words being approximations
anyway, and his tone not quite like
yelling "Fire!" in a crowded theater
but close.
        A moth drawing near
a flame supposedly symbolizes
the soul in its craving unable to
resist but just as likely might imply
a matter of misdirection.
                Directionless,
people still end up somewhere
in remote and unremote locales,
deserved and undeserved, leading
lives of quiet elation easily
accessible to those who want to
study another way out of wherever
they happen to be.
        Or not to be
is an apparent option, but wouldn't
that be a slight version compared
to walking a small town sidewalk
amid struck poses of mannequins
in thought?
        An hour of being mindless
feels like not being able to say what
being feels like, assuming it has
a frisson, as an interval has facets,
as a beginning or ending has a quality
that can't be touched.
        O hearers,
what are we to do with this elusive
sense of making progress toward

abiding within each other's thoughts,
getting only as close as the clock
hand gets to the moment farther out
ahead,
      already leaving us behind.

STRAY SURMISES

Instead of searching, why can't
we overhear wisdom, as if all we
needed were to sit beneath an oak
wind-shivering, sending down leaf
after leaf into our laps, each picked
up and examined.
                    A theme begins
to emerge but requires everyone—
including those from history
and those not born yet—just to
be glimpsed and even then not
agreed upon.
                    Call such days
glorious, even so, since silence
abounds with theories and invitations
into something purer, something
unforeseen but apt.
                    We could accept,
in a less sentient way, an argument
made by ruts appearing when rain
begins, how something we might
call *flow* follows its own logic
it does no good to try to refute
or disbelieve.
                    A few stray surmises
persist all one's life, nothing much
to build on but oddly beautiful
and bold and occasionally brazen,
maybe even necessary in the end,
though not "of" the end.
                    Assuredly,
the proper transitions will come, will
connect the pebble to the mountain,
the beach to the sunset, the twilight
to something that prevails—even

if unthinkable by all the thinkers
trying to articulate the ghost-dances
of their moods' subsidings, of the stream
thought tries to be, always muddied by
the least stirring,
                    less and less flowing on...

QUESTIONS TO BEGIN A DAY WITH

Memory ought to come with some disclaimers,
at least a mourner or two following in its
wake, calling attention to the intersection
between realism and how the mind only
occasionally has origins one can stand in
or trace.
        A lot of doodling, we may discover,
serves as underpinning—as do broodings,
sighs, empty fields outside of town, the fact
the evening rain sometimes carries over
into morning.
            That living has loopholes
we slip through—finding another path
to be on for a while—proves how
dwellingly the soul goes on listening
to a shadow reaching part way inside
a church door.
            Am I really here? and
How many unanswerables exist?
are but two questions to begin a day
with, to interject into conversations,
which are a recourse to something
within us forever hidden from ourselves
and others.
            Uncertain on sidewalks
could be written above our foreheads
as we meander toward each other's
faces, trespassing lines there, the upward
looks, the words we want to breathe
for how they grant a self we're being
summoned to or wake up looking
out from,
            inviting others in, inward.

OTHER OPTIONS FOR UNDERSTANDING

Certain words form how one speaks
— generously, nudgingly—as if,
in order to visit a friend, one takes
the same path through the woods
each time, content, if need be,
to get lost.
        That professor who
kept saying *in many ways* but
never elaborated so that you had
the sense that more existed but
would never find the full weight
of any one detail.
        Or the preacher saying
in a sense, which you misheard as
innocence, knowing, even if you lived
a millennium, you'd never experience
feeling like a child again not knowing
the world isn't merciful.
        You wonder
how often *the self as a construct* has
entered your own mind, crowding out
other options for understanding who you
are or might become.
        Then, for no
reason you can follow or find a way
back into, you think of a barn on a road
you used to drive daily, the harrowing
lean the loft seemed about to relinquish
but not yet, not for decade, not with
a few cows nearby,
        heads bent, being fed.

ONE KNOWING BEGINNING AS ANOTHER ENDS

I never purported to know the whole thing,
scarcely even a portion of it, though I
rejoiced exploring trails that went so far
and then stopped.
                    How one *knowing* begins
as another ends will always be, I suppose,
of concern to a few souls bent on interpreting
implications and subtle shifts, as if an outline
might be drawn, or redrawn, or, when necessary,
altogether abandoned.
                        An attempt to embrace,
or even to make allowances for, several possible
outcomes is seldom condoned, rarely admired,
never heralded; but if we're going to be about
the business of defining things, we should add
this trait to what we think we know concerning
generosity.
            The woods' falling leaves aren't stingy
with where they give themselves to the earth,
here or there, singly or together, next to a log
or inches from where a field begins; and neither
should we be, for our own bodies are just as
easily ripped from whatever high place we
think ourselves safe.
                        Not that a state of peril
should be assumed; not that catastrophes
await us, some fortuitous, others logical;
not that mishaps and hazards beckon our words,
but I doubt the present tense has room for us,
and not a song we know can alter
                                    the unchanging
nature of what is
                    to what we hope *hope* could be,
seeing it daily weaken its grip, becoming less

interested in pursuing what clearly now will never be
revealed
    but will, despite all angles attempted, remain hidden.

INTO OTHER LIGHT AS YET UNSPENT

Now that the day's been clearly
held and breathed in, what more
"voice" will be necessary to
carry us forth into other light
as yet unspent?
            So few reasons
are needed, though I'm always
attentive to ones I happen upon
just in case some gentleness
in me needs to respond or be
canceled out.
            Afterwards, logistics
get muddled in murmured amendments
the wise keep doling out in aphoristic
tones.
        How shall I unassume all
I'm certain of, as if any of it has
lead me to here, not to mention
all I'm uncertain of, which surely
accounts for why I place twigs
on streams and watch them ripple
away.
        And how, often, reading
the word *eucalyptus*, I pause
to live inside its vowels, each
a universe and I merely a star
among the numberless, far-flung
silences.
          In asking what I want,
I hope to take in how one tree
leans against another in a free-fall
that hasn't happened yet but offers
the kind of image every writer
tries describing in a notebook
but rarely uses.

When I wake
at five, the night's not finished
introducing stars to steeples, which
begs the question of what other
conversations could be happening
too soon interrupted.
                    Answers,
how do you taste on your own tongue,
for when I say you, the hummingbird
is always lifting into the depths of
sky
      too soon always only itself.

WHERE ONE TRIED TO BE

Must opportunities, when they appear,
be almost always missed, one's
name fumbled or misheard,
a passing car backfiring at just
the moment the moment's crescendo
attempts fullness?
                    An emptiness
of sauntering along solemn streets
that might have been one's own
but, as life would have it, became
another's—well, there's that and,
as Benn says, what to make of one's
nihilism.
                    Finding meaning's purpose,
though arduous, was once where one tried
to dwell, even if all that emerged were circling
swifts, an outstretched arm, the humor of
thinking the gesture might actually entice
some lone bird tired of beating furiously for
nowhere.
                    Each thought going somewhere
—even this thought—pulls all the others
forward, attempts a reckoning, finds
more steps in a pursuit seemingly getting
nowhere closer.
                    After years, one is farther
than ever from the place one started toward,
as if a decade-long endeavor had turned
excursion, errand, stroll and, absent any
markers, one were now left to stare up into
trees,
            one's placement down amid flowers.

THE WHOLE ENTERPRISE

Though anyone can say anything
and find believers, others caution
that such an approach might not
move us forward, while a few prefer
not speaking at all.
                    Maybe the matter
is more a pageantry of selves, some
too obvious to be convinced by; a few
undone; others annoying or archetypal,
too ambiguous to follow; or maybe
the matter is that the whole enterprise
lacks spirit.
                    An oeuvre of years is coming
to a close, something to brood upon, even
if no takers are present, busy elsewhere
being bewildered or narrowed down to
a single mood.
                    Meanwhile, thoughts begin
stacking up, too numerous to see in some
totality; and if there is a comfort to be found,
a summer road winding forth onto a plateau,
it never comes; and all the people commit
to memory
                    a word not shared with anyone else.

SOMEONE SPEAKING

Someone, even today, goes on speaking to his city,
while the walking hordes fold and infold, swerve, veer,
sway, thrum—honey-words maybe, full of concentration
for shops and coffee vendors, the ones who sweep
sidewalks.
        Someone else speaking to a tree, to wind,
and another to evening light beyond the ridge,
and one to the soul, to the bee on the bloom,
to fish in winter, to daybreak, to questions,
to snow lifting down.
            What is her name,
the one who speaks to the crook of a tree
where she left a message when she was ten,
having climbed to find a quiet place her parents
did not know?
        Someone goes on speaking, probing,
praising, pressing against, goes on building up
and tearing down,
          even if no one eavesdrops,
even if words are an absence and the absence
the only way
        to make her presence known.

HOW FAR AWAY WE ARE

As one day folds into another, how are
we to follow its unraveling edges, and
what authority would we find if we
bound them together?
                    "I'll follow the sun,"
McCartney claimed, and maybe we should
stand around repeating his claim in harmony
until a part of us can't contain itself and
moves into the next room where a blue
chair waits.
            How far away are we, really,
from home, from searching, from forgiveness,
from nothing more to say, from austerity,
from what we have not known or did not
know we needed to know?
                        Everything turns out
completely different than expected, although
with enough leisure and time, even a man
on a road at night gets to where he's going,
deepening the conversations in rooms where
people sing his arrival.
                        Are we understanding
something else now? Are we living already
in another life, in another region, where time
implies that nothing ever need be disquieting
again?
        Mountains live another state away, but
they also might be suppositions a child believes
for years, only to come upon one day as an old
man in his travels, only then to remember his
small self back there in the past still whispering
prayers,
            shade upon hue upon shadow receding.

MOMENTARY CLARITY

The church bells start amid two doves
fluttering back to flight, and this image
I take to be a momentary clarity gifted
into the world.
         There are things that
happen, though, that remain unnamable
just as a person speaking is actually
an amalgam of other voices, a word
or phrase, a tone which no one quite
can place.
         Should we be assured by this
or reassured or reassessed, and what are
the rules to govern what happens next
or what doesn't happen but still exerts
an influence?
         What can we actually *be*
certain of, since in one moment brakes
screech and in the next a fox slinks midway
out across a field, and the moments overlap,
sometimes amplifying a presence of sky
and other times abolishing each other,
duet then solo, tree branch swaying
then empty.
         Few things are more welcome
than having a window with an aesthetic,
a slight waviness to slide the scene
or else to ripple the bark of the maple
and the blue swing no one thinks
to sit in any more.
         Something needs done,
must be done, must be accomplished
even if all the streets refuse to pause,
the STOP signs voicing elegies, even if

amnesty has been offered none can hear
and all truths we've taken to ourselves
are just the ones
                    most easy to believe.

ONE OR ANOTHER FATE MOSTLY FORGOTTEN

We think we've finally solved how
to go about what remains of our
lives, but as soon as something in
the foreground comes clear, something
else steps forth in the distance,
and there's really no way to hold
both in mind.
                    Weary, the body
just gives up, settles into an afternoon's
lull and, in some traditions, must be
denied, castigated, cast aside, so as
not to be tempted past one's ability
to restrain the self.
                    Always there are other
lives to imagine with their own narrow
alleyways, lost door keys, lockets misplaced,
one or another fate mostly forgotten,
constituting what amounts to something
similar to what one has grown used to,
if not accepted.
                    Is enlightenment ever rejected,
ever experienced as an embarrassment,
ever sensed as an unraveling of a long
cherished belief?
                    What we do with doubt
is use it as a starting point, rhyming
more and more we meet in the world,
not to reject outright the codes we're
taught
          but to learn how to unlearn
what isn't necessary, or what becomes
distracting, or what happens when
promises made
                    one by one begin to unmake
explanations,
                    giving them back into mysteries.

ABOUT THE AUTHOR

Jeff Hardin is the author of five previous collections, most recently *Small Revolution* and *No Other Kind of World*. His work has been honored with the Nicholas Roerich Prize, the Donald Justice Poetry Prize, and the X. J. Kennedy Poetry Prize. His poems have appeared in *The Southern Review, Hudson Review, North American Review, Gettysburg Review, Southern Poetry Review,* and many others. He is a professor of English at Columbia State Community College in Tennessee. Visit his website at www.jeffhardin.weebly.com.

CPSIA information can be obtained
at www.ICGtesting.com
Printed in the USA
JSHW010114030819
1028JS00003B/12